YUMMI YOGHURT

– A First Taste of Stock Market Investment!

by

John Lee
Lord Lee of Trafford DL FCA

Grosvenor House
Publishing Limited

This book is published by
Grosvenor House Publishing Ltd
Link House
140 The Broadway, Tolworth, Surrey, KT6 7HT.
www.grosvenorhousepublishing.co.uk

A CIP record for this book
is available from the British Library

ISBN 978-1-78623-520-6

"Bite-sized lessons in the art of Stock-picking from one of the UK's best-known Small Cap investors."

Claer Barrett, Personal Finance Editor,
Financial Times

"Most students when they leave school have little knowledge of the world of business - what's a dividend, a flotation, a takeover, a unit trust or 'going public'? So John Lee an experienced and successful investor who writes for *FT Money* has written a beginner's guide to the world of finance, business and investment. This is the chronicle of a family business which grows from a clever idea to a company with worldwide sales. It is a route that many have travelled and John Lee has created the signposts along the way for others to follow."

Lord Kenneth Baker, former Education Secretary

"An essential read for anyone who wants to understand the world of investments. Plain-talking in plain English. Devour and learn how to build long-term wealth."

Jeff Prestridge, Personal Finance Editor,
The Mail on Sunday

"To my knowledge, a first on Stock Market investment for teenagers. Investing in and supporting business growth is socially useful - helping to create jobs and wealth. Indeed "Yummi Yoghurt" is an excellent investment in itself!"

Gervais Williams, Managing Director, Miton Group

DEDICATION

To my Grandchildren,
Eli, Florence, Isaac and Ivan
Hoping that at least one of them will inherit my enthusiasm for
The Stock Market!

CONTENTS

ACKNOWLEDGEMENTS

With grateful thanks to:

Robbie Cathro for the cover illustration and
Kate Wakeham for her help with design and art direction

The Economics Department and Students of
Withington Girls' School

My secretary, Kathy Fogarty, for all secretarial back-up

The Team at Grosvenor House Publishing for
facilitating this publication

and finally, to the very many colleagues and friends,
and their families, who have offered guidance,
suggestions and support.

INTRODUCTION

I bought my first shares when I was fifteen – over sixty years ago – investing £45 in shipping company Aviation & Shipping who owned one ship. Sadly, the vessel foundered taking all my investment with it! Not the most auspicious start to my investing life!

Looking back, my early investment knowledge was almost literally gained on my medical father's shoulder as he sat crossed-legged on the floor in his library, smoking his favourite pipe, pouring over copies of the then-weekly publications *The Investor's Chronicle* (still going today) and *The Stock Exchange Gazette*. As I started to delve myself into these publications and talk with him I became increasingly fascinated and captivated by the Stock Market and the worlds of investment and public companies. Over the years investing became a core interest and activity of mine. I am passionate about encouraging people, particularly the young, to become investors themselves and to share the pleasure and hopefully the profitable experiences that I have had (we all make mistakes!). However, I have long felt that there was a need for a first-stage easy-to-read guide to Stock Market investment for beginners – I only wish there had been such a publication when I started all those years ago. Hence this book *Yummi Yoghurt* was conceived to fill the gap. It tells the story of a Devon farming family who started producing yoghurt to supplement their farm income, which developed into a very successful business ultimately becoming a publicly quoted company, and how the teenage children of another family made their first ever investments in Yummi, when it went public, using monies left to them by their grandfather.

What the Stock Exchange is, how to buy and sell shares, dividends, comparative valuations etc., are all covered, as are the reasons why shares may rise and fall. Yummi is not intended to be a comprehensive guide to Stock Market investment – what it is intended to do is to give the beginner a basic "feel" and understanding of investment – to whet the appetite – which should at the very least enable the reader to broadly understand city media articles and the language of stockbrokers, financial advisers and wealth-managers. In short, it introduces the reader to investment in a light, easy-to-read, undemanding way, and encouraging more people to save and invest surely has to be in our national interest as well.

THE STORY OF YUMMI YOGHURT
From Dairy Farm to Public Company

It had been a very happy day. The new purpose built Yummi Yoghurt factory had been officially opened by the Mayor, supported by the Member of Parliament. Regional TV and representatives from the two supermarket groups, on whose firm contracts the Baron family had felt confident enough to borrow from the bank to finance the new factory, had all been there. With the ceremony over, all present including the families of their 40 employees tucked into a lavish buffet. What had started out five years ago as a fun venture, utilising Tessa Baron's culinary skills, and as a way to diversify and supplement their modest Devon farm family income, had grown into a serious commercial venture. Husband Reg was now in charge of purchasing and transport, and daughter Fiona – who had just graduated in business administration – had control of the finances. The previous week they had met with their accountants to discuss results for the last financial year. After directors' salaries and all other costs they were showing a profit of just over £50,000! Yummi Yoghurt was really up and running – high quality, low fat fruit yoghurts from their West Country base.

Ten years later the business had gone from strength-to-strength. Turnover (sales) had soared to £9 million, their workforce was now 100 strong, a new factory extension had just been completed and they were supplying many of the country's major supermarket chains. Father Reg was now part-time Chairman, Mum Tessa a very hands-on Managing

Director, Fiona, now married, had moved to Marketing Director with her husband Jeremy (a chartered accountant) as Financial Director and Company Secretary.

In recent years they had received a number of takeover approaches from major national food manufacturing groups, but had rejected them all, wishing to remain independent, develop at their own pace, and above all maintain product quality. They believed that they had many years of growth still ahead. Yummi had now become quite a valuable business and on the advice of their accountants the family decided to consider their future options in conjunction with a recommended leading investment bank, Carstairs & Co.

Put very simply, the figures which they showed to the Carstairs team were:

Forecast sales:		£ 9,000,000
Less costs of sales, ingredients, packaging, staff wages etc.	£3,600,000	
Overheads, heat, light, transportation etc.	£ 900,000	£ 4,500,000
Profit before tax:		£ 4,500,000
Corporation Tax at 20%		£ 900,000
Net profit after tax:		£ 3,600,000

The Balance Sheet of Yummi was as follows:

Freehold property	£ 4,000,000	Yummi's factory in Devon
Plant equipment, vehicles	£ 1,500,000	
Stock	£ 500,000	Raw materials, packaging ingredients
Debtors	£ 2,000,000	Goods sold to customers e.g. supermarkets not yet paid for
Cash in the bank	£ 2,500,000	
Total Assets	£10,500,000	
Less Creditors	£ 500,000	Amounts Yummi owes
Net Assets	£10,000,000	

Represented by say 10,000,000 shares of £1 each £10,000,000
The Net Asset Value is the difference between the total assets of £10,500,000 and the total liabilities of £500,000 = £10,000,000.

Thus each share had a Net Asset Value of £1

Yummi was a cash-generative business, such that the Barons had more than repaid all the original money borrowed for a new factory five years ago, indeed they now had over £2 million in the bank!

So, the family were in a very comfortable financial position. However virtually all their wealth outside their original farm, which was now more of a hobby, was tied-up in the Yummi business. Having carefully considered matters Reg and Tessa felt that as they were 65 and 60 respectively, it would be nice if for the first time in their lives they could take some capital out of Yummi, and perhaps buy a holiday/retirement home in France which had always been a far-off dream. Having taken everything into account, Yummi's history, its accounts, its product reputation and future prospects, Carstairs recommended that the Barons should consider taking Yummi "public" i.e. selling a proportion of its share capital to outside investors while retaining control of the business. This course of action would allow Reg and Tessa to take some money out of the business – the proceeds of their shares they sold to the wider public.

Carstairs were now in the driving seat having been appointed by the family to handle and advise on the flotation. They recommended that Yummi should "go public" early next year giving eight months to prepare. On Carstairs advice, the Baron family decided to replace their West County solicitors and accountants with major national firms and also to appoint a financial public relations firm. They didn't find it easy to break the news to their local professional firms, but explained it was necessary, on the advice of Carstairs, to appoint firms better known and respected by potential new investors. However, the Barons assured them that they would continue to handle the family's personal taxation and legal affairs. It was explained to the Barons that although the financial PR firm was expensive it was important to plan a media campaign for the next few months – generating awareness of Yummi and its products, and its intention to obtain a public quotation – hopefully whetting potential investors' appetites to consider applying for Yummi shares when they become available.

During the year the family had a number of meetings with Carstairs, their new auditors and solicitors, and the financial PR firm together with their newly-appointed stockbrokers, all of whom would be involved in the flotation. Having discussed timing options with the Stock Exchange, the flotation was fixed for the last week of the following January. Immediately after Christmas Carstairs got down to deciding on the price that Yummi shares should be sold at, studying particularly the share prices of other quoted food manufacturing companies and also taking into account the general level of the Stock Market. Carstairs advised that there were two main options for Yummi to go public: there could either be an "Offer For Sale" with a prospectus in the national press, which would deliver the equivalent of a full-page advertisement setting out comprehensive details on Yummi – names of directors, professional advisers, financial history, the balance sheet, and a forecast of future turnover and profits, plus a projected dividend. A dividend is the amount of profits, after the payment of Corporation Tax, that the company's directors decide could and should be paid out to shareholders. In making this decision they would take into account the future financial needs of the business i.e. are they planning to buy new modern plant and equipment or perhaps, say, the next generation of computers or robots, to enable the business to become more efficient. The other option Carstairs explained is to go public by a "placing" whereby a company's shares are "placed" with investors i.e. institutions or private investors via Stockbrokers. A Stockbroking firm is one whose business is the buying and selling of shares – parts of companies – on behalf of institutions i.e. insurance companies, pension funds etc., and individual private investors.

The share capital of Yummi was now £10 million divided into 10 million shares of £1 each. It was decided that the Barons would sell 40% of their shares in the flotation leaving them with 60% – thus still firmly in control. It was jointly agreed after much discussion that they would go down the "Offer For Sale" route. Their thinking was that as Yummi was a consumer product, an Offer For Sale would provide much more publicity than a placing, so adding to customer awareness – hopefully resulting in even more sales of Yummi Yoghurt! It was also agreed that the shares should be attractively priced to generate significant public/investor interest. The last thing they wanted was a "flop" – all shares on offer not being applied for – which obviously would reflect badly on the company's image and reputation.

Having taken all factors into account, it was finally agreed that Yummi's shares should be offered for sale at a price for £3 for a £1 share, thus giving an overall valuation for Yummi of £30 million i.e. 10 million shares at £3 each. The Baron family's 60% holding would consequently be worth £18 million – making them multi-millionaires!

The Prospectus for the "Offer for Sale" would contain a forecast:

Sales	£10,000,000
Less cost of sales	£ 5,000,000
Profit before Tax	£ 5,000,000
Less 20% Corporation Tax	£ 1,000,000
Net Profit:	£ 4,000,000

It was decided that half of the profits should be retained in the business for further expansion and new automated production lines etc., leaving £2 million for dividends to shareholders. This would be the equivalent of a 20% dividend on each of the 10 million shares. Therefore, at the flotation price of £3 a share the dividend yield is calculated as follows:

$$\frac{\text{Nominal value of Yummi shares}}{\text{Market Price}} \times 20\%$$

$$\text{i.e. } \frac{\pounds 1}{\pounds 3} \times 20\% = 6.66\%$$

(Put another way, anyone investing £100 would be buying 33 shares at £3 each. Thus, with a 20% dividend they would receive £6.60.) Frequently a dividend is declared in pence per share, thus the 20% dividend could be expressed as 20p per £1 share. As can be seen, the £2 million cost of dividends is covered twice by the available £4 million of net profit.

At £3 per share the Price Earnings Ratio – a valuation for comparing share prices – was 7.5 calculated as follows:

Total Market Capitalisation: £30,000,000

$$\div \quad = 7.5$$

Post Tax Profits: £4,000,000

The Stock Exchange

The Stock Exchange is basically like any other market – an opportunity to buy or sell things or goods. Just as Smithfield is a market for meat and Billingsgate a market for fish, the Stock Exchange is a market where parts or shares of businesses are bought and sold on behalf of institutions or individuals by banks or stockbrokers. Essentially it provides a mechanism for businesses to raise money from shareholders for development and expansion. Most businesses in the UK are private companies i.e. owned privately by individuals or families. It is public companies – usually but not necessarily larger businesses – where the general public, you and me, can buy and sell shares. It is not only individuals who may own shares, they can also be held by institutions e.g. insurance companies or pension funds, or other funds. Many individuals instead of owning shares in their own right prefer to invest via funds i.e., Investment Trusts or Unit Trusts. These are essentially collective vehicles where the monies of private investors are blocked together, with the fund itself owning the shares in those public companies. There are a whole range of funds to invest in – many for example specialising in different parts of the world i.e. the First India Fund, as its name implies, only investing in companies quoted in India, while say the Blue Cross Health Fund might only invest in Healthcare businesses. Investing through such a fund helps to spread risk rather than the risk inherent in investing directly in a particular company.

The Jennings Family

Mark, a solicitor, and Lesley, a dentist, live just outside Bury, Lancashire, with their 18-year-old son Ben and twin 16-year-old daughters, Melanie and Helen. With both parents working professionally, the Jennings family are comfortably-off financially, with their house mortgage long since paid-off and having built-up a joint share portfolio – mainly "Large Cap" stocks i.e. shares in national or international companies. Father Mark had mentioned the Stock Market to his three children – none of them had so far shown much interest! However last Christmas their Grandfather – Lesley's father – died leaving £2,500 to each of his grandchildren. Ben decided to spend £1,000 on a second-hand car having just passed his test, but Melanie and Helen decided to save their windfall. Over the dinner table the family discussed their financial options – each child favoured Premium Bonds, but Mark was hoping to encourage them to think about the Stock Market. He had read newspaper reports that Yummi Yoghurt was "going public" and was aware that the whole family enjoyed their yoghurt brands. What better way to encourage the youngsters to invest than to point them towards acquiring a shareholding in Yummi!

On the Monday of the last week in January the prospectus (Offer for Sale) appeared in two national daily papers. 40% of the shares in Yummi were offered for sale at £3 per share. The minimum number that could be applied for was 100 – it was stated that if the offer was oversubscribed i.e. the public applied for more shares than were on offer – then those applying for a smaller number of shares would be favoured – those applying for larger numbers would be scaled back. The reasoning behind this was that with Yummi being a consumer product, the more shareholders there were the greater likelihood of developing awareness and loyalty of and to the Yummi brand.

Press comment on the Offer for Sale was universally favourable. Most commentators knew the product, there was no other sole UK yoghurt manufacturer in which one could invest, (most other quality yoghurt manufacturers being part of larger food manufacturing groups) and the terms – a PER of 7.5 and a dividend yield of 6.6% were considered very attractive. In addition, commentators agreed that Yummi offered considerable growth prospects – not only was the sale of yoghurt growing year-on-year, but Yummi had stated in their prospectus that they were developing a number of new related dairy products, some of which were to be launched in the New Year.

The Jennings family bought extra copies of the newspaper which contained the Yummi prospectus on the day it appeared. Ben, Melanie and Helen had all decided to apply for 200 shares each. Father Mark checked each of their application forms carefully, ensuring that the £600 cheques etc., (200 x £3 per share) were correctly filled-in. They all eagerly awaited Friday's announcement of the results of the Offer for Sale: Great News! A Huge Success – in total investors had applied for ten times the number of shares being sold – in City parlance it had been "over-subscribed" ten times.

It was announced that larger applications were being drastically scaled-down so that anyone applying for 500 shares or less would receive their full requirement. The three Jennings children were delighted – they would receive the 200 shares they had each applied for; Mark and Lesley breathed a joint sigh of relief that so far at least their attempt to encourage Stock Market investment by their offspring had gone smoothly.

Now on to the following Tuesday when dealings in Yummi shares were due to start on the Stock Exchange! The whole family was excited. Lesley checked at 8:00am – the moment of first dealings – a great "Yippee!" went up. Yummi shares had opened at £3.60 each, 20% higher than the £3 offer price. So, all three children each had £720 worth of Yummi shares – on paper a profit of £120 on their £600 outlay. This premium meant that the whole of Yummi was now valued at £36 million – a 20% rise on the original £30 million. This new valuation meant that the PE ratio which had been 7.5 i.e.:

$$£30,000,000 ÷ £4,000,000 \text{ after tax profits} = 7.5$$

Was now:

$$£36,000,000 ÷ £4,000,000 \text{ after tax profits} = 9$$

The dividend yield, which had been 6.66% at £3 per share was now down to:

$$\frac{£1}{£3.60} × 20\% = 5.6\%$$

The Baron Family had given all their employees with over one year's service 250 shares each as a gift, so they were delighted too!

Ten Reasons Why Yummi shares might rise

1. Yummi delivers increased profits and dividends year-on-year.
2. Favourable press comment.
3. Other supermarkets etc., start taking Yummi products.
4. A general rise in most share prices on the Stock Market.
5. Yummi announce a new range of dairy products.
6. Rumours of a takeover bid for Yummi i.e. another company is suggested as being interested in buying them.
7. A well-regarded private investor or institution i.e. insurance company or pension fund buys a large number of shares.
8. Optimistic comment by Yummi directors on future prospects.
9. Yummi shares upwardly re-rated (see later explanation).
10. Statistical evidence of increased national sales of yoghurt.

Ten Reasons Why Yummi shares might fall

1. Yummi's profits fall.
2. Yummi reduces (cuts) its dividend.
3. A general fall in share prices because of world events.
4. The Baron Family sell a large percentage of their shares.
5. There is a contamination/health scare regarding Yummi's products.
6. A major supermarket chain delists (stops selling) Yummi products.
7. Unfavourable press comment.
8. Key executive(s) or professional advisors resign or are charged with an offence.
9. Significant rise in the cost of ingredients/cartons/packaging etc.
10. A substantial long-term Yummi shareholder sells all or part of their holding.

Price Earnings Ratios

In our story, at the time of the Offer for Sale, Yummi was valued on a PER of 7.5 i.e.

CAPITALISATION   £30,000,000 ÷ = 7.5
AFTER TAX PROFITS (Earnings)   £ 4,000,000

On the first day of dealings as a public company with the shares rising from £3 to £3.60, its PER had risen to 9 i.e.

CAPITALISATION   £36,000,000 ÷ = 9
AFTER TAX PROFITS (Earnings) £ 4,000,000

Consequently the upward movement in Yummi's shares had delivered an increase in the Price Earnings Ratio from 7.5 to 9 i.e. valuing Yummi more highly (upwardly re-rating them).

If Yummi's shares were to rise to say £4 then the PER would go even higher:

CAPITALISATION   £10,000,000 x 4 = £40,000,000 ÷ =10
AFTER TAX PROFITS (Earnings)   £ 4,000,000

So the higher the Price Earnings Ratio, the more highly are investors valuing the business.

Some very highly valued shares can be on a PER of 50 plus i.e. where investors think that the growth prospects for rising profits etc., are outstandingly good.

Conversely other very lowly valued shares can be on a 5 PER or similar i.e. where investors think that profits have very limited growth prospects, or indeed might fall, or perhaps its dividend might be reduced, or borrowings (debt) dangerously high.

It can be seen that the PER, at any one time, is an indication of how investors assess a company's prospects – comparison being made between different companies on the basis of their Price Earnings Ratios. It is only one of a number of yardsticks which are used to compare the valuations of different public companies.

Ben Jennings recounted the story of his Yummi investment to his closest college friend, Sanjay Karim. He had never invested in shares before but had built up savings in his bank account. Following discussions at his bank branch, they indicated that they would be happy to introduce him to local Bury Stockbrokers James Sharp and Co. Sanjay decided to invest himself in Yummi even though the market price had risen from £3 to £3.60. The actual quote of Yummi shares was £3.50–£3.60 i.e. an investor could sell shares at £3.50 or buy at £3.60. The difference being the market-maker's 'turn' or profit. He decided to buy 100 shares and received a 'Bought' contract note as follows:

James Sharp & Co.
The Exchange
5 Bank Street
Bury Lancashire BL9 0DN

Tel : 0161 764 4043
Fax : 0161 764 1628
DX : 20536 Bury
E : mail@jamessharp.co.uk

WWW.JAMESSHARP.CO.UK

Partners
Ian Bolton Chartered FCSI
Michael Tulip ACA, Chartered FCSI
Martin Entwistle BA (Hons), Chartered FCSI

Associate
Stephen Ross Chartered FCSI

Authorised and regulated
by the Financial Conduct
Authority

Member of the
London Stock Exchange

Member of Nexexchange

Member of PIMFA

JAMES SHARP & Co.

Sanjay Karim	**Client Ref**	S1234
Hillside View	**Contract No.**	74B
Bury	**Date**	28/03/2019 **Time** 10.00
Lancashire	**Settlement Day**	04/04/2019
BY6 PQ	**Stock Code**	X775463

We thank you for your instructions and have this day	BOUGHT

Yummi Yoghurt Plc
£1 Ordinary Shares

Quantity	Price	Bargain Conditions	Amount
100	360p		360.00
		Commission	22.00
		Compliance Charge	10.00
		Total	392.00

Notes: Contract notes should be retained for tax purposes.
We have acted as agents on your behalf in this transaction unless otherwise specified.
This contract is issued subject to the Rules and Regulations of the London Stock Exchange and to our normal terms and conditions of business.
Any errors or omissions should be reported immediately to your Account Executive.
Best execution cannot be guaranteed for transactions effected outside official market hours.

IMPORTANT SETTLEMENT INSTRUCTIONS

Client Ref	Bargain Ref	Settlement Date	Total Consideration
S1234	74B	04/04/2019	392.00

PURCHASES Please detach this slip and return it together with your cheque to be received by us no later than **three business days** prior to the settlement date indicated above. Alternatively, please make arrangements to transfer funds to the following account, quoting your client reference. James Sharp & Co Client Deposit, The Royal Bank Of Scotland, 40 The Rock, Bury, A/C No. 11175859, Sort Code 16-15-12, IBAN GB83RBOS16151211175859, SWIFT/BIC RBOSGB2L PLEASE IGNORE SETTLEMENT REQUIREMENTS FOR ISA PURCHASES

SALES Please detach this slip and return it together with the completed transfer form and relevant certificate to be received by us no later than **three business days** prior to the settlement date indicated above.

CP MAR 2018 Ref JSP

Thus Sanjay's total cost, after Broker's charges, was £392

At the end of each financial year every Public Company has to publish an 'Annual Report,' a copy of which must be sent to every shareholder, and should also be available on its website. Annual Reports contain a mass of detailed information e.g. names and backgrounds of directors, a list of its professional advisors, reports usually from the Chairman and Chief Executive covering the financial results for the past year, usually comments on current trading and future prospects, and what dividend (if any) is recommended. The report will also contain a Profit and Loss Account and Balance Sheet, certified and approved by the appointed Auditors (firms of accountants whose job it is to confirm the accuracy of the financial accounts). The Annual Report will also usually contain a formal notice of the company's Annual General Meeting, which public companies are required to hold each year. Twenty-one-days' notice has to be given of this meeting which is open to all shareholders to attend. This gives individual shareholders an opportunity to question Directors on the company's activities and results etc. and meet with them usually after the formal meeting has closed. Yummi always provided pots of yoghurt at their Annual General Meeting for shareholders to taste, plus a small pack to take away!

At the meeting a number of formal resolutions are usually put to shareholders:

1. To approve the Annual Report and Accounts.
2. To re-appoint certain Directors (Directors retire by rotation and have to be re-appointed by shareholders).
3. To confirm the re-appointment of X, Y, and Z Chartered Accountants as Auditors of the company for coming financial year.
4. To approve the dividend recommended by the Directors.

After the AGM dividend warrants (cheques) will be sent out to each qualifying shareholder – the amount they receive being obviously dependent on the number of shares they own and the rate of dividend paid per share.

Three years later Melanie, now 19-years-old, decided to use her gap year before starting a veterinary course to travel to the Far East. To finance her trip, she decided to sell half her Yummi holding. During these last years, Yummi had delivered outstanding growth – profits nearly doubling to £7 million after tax, and with the original 20% dividend now at a 40% level. Unsurprisingly the shares which she had bought at £3 had now risen to £8 reflecting this performance and were being valued more highly by investors. As a result the Price Earnings Ratio was:

Share Capital 10,000,000 x £8 = £80,000,000 (Capitalisation)

÷

£ 7,000,000 (after tax profits)

= 11.5 approx.

The Dividend Yield at £8, and with a 40% dividend, was now:

$\dfrac{£1}{£8}$ × 40 = 5%   (i.e. anyone investing £100 in Yummi shares would receive a Dividend of £5)

Melanie contacted the family's Stockbrokers, James Sharp of Bury – her parents had been clients for many years, so she needed no real introduction, and instructed them to sell half of her holding – 100 shares at the best price. They first of all sent her a new client's application form to complete, and on its return duly signed, they carried out her instructions. The Stock Market quote for Yummi was £8 to sell. Melanie received a "Sale" contract note from the Stockbrokers as follows:

YUMMI YOGHURT

James Sharp & Co.
The Exchange
5 Bank Street
Bury Lancashire BL9 0DN

Tel : 0161 764 4043
Fax : 0161 764 1628
DX : 20536 Bury
E : mail@jamessharp.co.uk

WWW.JAMESSHARP.CO.UK

Partners
Ian Bolton Chartered FCSI
Michael Tulip ACA, Chartered FCSI
Martin Entwistle BA (Hons), Chartered FCSI

Associate
Stephen Ross Chartered FCSI

Authorised and regulated
by the Financial Conduct
Authority
Member of the
London Stock Exchange
Member of Nexexchange
Member of PIMFA

JAMES SHARP & Co.

Ms Melanie Jennings	
'The Coppice'	
Last Drop Road	
Bury	
Lancashire	
BY6 RT	

Client Ref	J1435
Contract No.	100C
Date	21/01/2020
Settlement Day	24/01/2020
Stock Code	X775463

Time
11.00

We thank you for your instructions and have this day | **SOLD**

Yummi Yoghurt Plc
£1 Ordinary Shares

Quantity	Price	Bargain Conditions	Amount
100	800p		800.00
		Commission	22.00
		Compliance Charge	10.00
		Total	768.00

Notes: Contract notes should be retained for tax purposes.
We have acted as agents on your behalf in this transaction unless otherwise specified.
This contract is issued subject to the Rules and Regulations of the London Stock Exchange and to our normal
terms and conditions of business.
Any errors or omissions should be reported immediately to your Account Executive.
Best execution cannot be guaranteed for transactions effected outside official market hours.

- -

IMPORTANT SETTLEMENT INSTRUCTIONS

Client Ref	Bargain Ref	Settlement Date	Total Consideration
J1435	100C	24/01/2020	768;00

PURCHASES   Please detach this slip and return it together with your cheque to be received by us no later than **three business days**
prior to the settlement date indicated above. Alternatively, please make arrangements to transfer funds to the following
account, quoting your client reference. James Sharp & Co Client Deposit, The Royal Bank Of Scotland, 40 The Rock, Bury,
A/C No. 11175859, Sort Code 16-15-12, IBAN GB83RBOS16151211175859, SWIFT/BIC RBOSGBZL
PLEASE IGNORE SETTLEMENT REQUIREMENTS FOR ISA PURCHASES

SALES   Please detach this slip and return it together with the completed transfer form and relevant certificate to be
received by us no later than **three business days** prior to the settlement date indicated above.

CP MAR 2018 Rel JSP

19

So, after the Stockbroker's commission and their compliance charge Melanie received a cheque for £768 – more than the original total £600 cost for her 200 shares – and she still had 100 shares left! How grateful she was to Yummi and of course to her parents for encouraging her to invest! Without the money from the sale Melanie could not have afforded her Far Eastern trip – she would have had to rely on borrowing the cost from her parents or finding a part-time job.

Melanie had done well to sell at £8 because the following year Yummi suffered its first set-back since "going public." Tiny fragments of glass were found in one of their yoghurt cartons by an Aberdeen customer. She had bought the carton at a local major supermarket outlet who immediately notified Yummi. It was agreed that all Yummi products produced in that batch would be withdrawn, not only from the supermarket concerned, but from all other supermarket chains and independent outlets as well. Yummi undertook to reimburse any customers who had bought yoghurt provided they returned the cartons to their store of purchase for destruction. In addition, total production was shut-down while all machinery and packaging lines were cleaned and carefully checked. Fortunately, no other glass fragments were found nor was their source ever traced. It was calculated that the whole incident cost Yummi £1 million in production stoppage, compensation and loss of sales. Parallel to the public announcement Yummi also had to make a formal announcement to the Stock Market which caused their shares to fall from the then £8.50 to £7. Yummi forecast that their annual profits, which had been expected to rise from £7 million to £8 million would now mark time at the lower figure. With no more contamination discovered and optimistic comments about a return to profits the following year, the share price gradually recovered to £8 by the year end.

Two years later i.e. five years from going public, Yummi received a "Takeover Bid" from a large multi-million-pound international food group, Global Foods Inc – keen to buy

Yummi and its brand to add a new product range to their existing portfolio of brands. Their initial offer was £11 per share, valuing Yummi at £110 million. The Directors' of Yummi – the Baron Family members who still effectively owned 60% of the share capital and their two "Independent" i.e. non-family Directors immediately entered into discussions with advisors Carstairs & Co. While profits of Yummi had now risen to £10 million the prospects for further growth were looking more limited given that all the major supermarket chains were already stocking their yoghurt/dairy products. In addition, Reg and Tessa Baron had effectively reached retirement age, and Fiona and Jeremy were keen to spend more time with their young family so the feeling was that if Yummi could obtain a higher bid then they would accept it provided the bidder committed to retain both the Devon factory and all their employees.

Following further discussions and the provision of more detailed information to the prospective bidder, the bid level was raised to £13 a share valuing Yummi at £130 million. Terms were agreed and the Board of Yummi pledged to accept the offer and recommend it to outside shareholders. Formal documents were sent out in due course to all shareholders including the Jennings Family. So, Ben and Helen who had each retained their 200 shares were going to receive £2,600 compared with their original outlay of £600 and Melanie, with 100 shares left, should receive £1,300 – all making very sizeable profits on their original purchase. Ben's close friend, Sanjay, was also delighted – receiving £13 a share against his £3.60 purchase price. The documentation gave them the option of having their proceeds paid directly into their bank accounts rather than receiving a cheque.

So, for Ben, Melanie and Helen – and also Sanjay – their first foray into the Stock Market had been a huge success. They were all now looking for their next investment opportunity and had started to explore the financial columns of national papers, company websites etc., and happily to discuss ideas and opportunities with their parents and their Stockbroker – all having become clients of their local Bury firm of James Sharp. But they must be careful. Yes, Yummi had been a great investment but all investment in businesses – public or private – carries a degree of risk and they would be very fortunate to easily find another Yummi. Indeed perhaps it would be sensible to only consider reinvesting half their Yummi proceeds, keeping the other half in the Bank or perhaps something very safe like Premium Bonds. Rather than re-invest in the shares of just one company, they might consider buying shares in, say, three different ones, to spread the risk and increase their investment knowledge of companies and sectors. Crucially, they must remember that all investors make mistakes and lose money from time-to-time – but the aim is of course to generate more profits than losses!

On the final page I list twelve key recommendations which hopefully will help readers/investors to reduce risks and avoid losses.

To conclude our story the Baron Family – still owning their 60% of Yummi received a whopping £78 million for their holding i.e., six million shares at £13 following the takeover. Reg and Tessa happily retired to France, Fiona and Jeremy who stayed in post for six months to facilitate the physical and human aspects of the takeover, continued to manage the family farm and made generous donations to their local church and to West Country charities. They focussed their energies on charitable work with Fiona also becoming a Governor of their local primary school. Ben Jennings, who found his Yummi investing experience so rewarding and exciting resolved to become a Stockbroker, while Melanie, Helen and Sanjay built up very useful share portfolios over the years. Yummi – having become part of Global Foods Inc., developed a substantial export business, benefitting from the greater resources and connections of its new owner. The Baron Family were delighted with the onward progress and expansion of Yummi as its factory was subsequently doubled in size, becoming one of the largest employers in the West Country.

This story demonstrates how the development and growth of a business benefits not only the founders and its shareholders, but also employees and the local and regional community. In Yummi's case employment opportunities in a rural area would obviously be limited, so a new growing manufacturing business providing jobs nearer to home would be very welcomed. In addition, of course, a growing business provides a significant outlet for local tradespeople and suppliers – from builders and electricians to taxi drivers and catering vendors. Finally, the national Exchequer benefits from Corporation Tax paid by companies like Yummi out of its profits, and the tax deductions and NI etc., contributions from their employees. A happy story with everyone a winner!

SUMMARY OVER YUMMI'S FIVE YEARS PUBLIC COMPANY LIFE

	PROFITS AFTER TAX	SHARE PRICE	PE RATIO	RATE OF DIVIDEND PAID
On flotation	£4,000,000	£3	7.5	20%
1st day of dealings as a public company	£4,000,000	£3.60	9	20%
Melanie sells half her shareholding	£7,000,000	£8	11.5 approx.	40%
Takeover agreed five years after flotation	£10,000,000	£13	13	50%

GLOSSARY
(In alphabetical order)

AIM (Alternative Investment Market)	A junior Market to the main Stock Market, generally preferred by relatively new or smaller companies, where regulations are less stringent and costs of "going public" lower. Many AIM shares also currently qualify for Inheritance Tax relief if held for a certain number of years.
BALANCE SHEET	A summary of what a business owns and what is owes.
CAPITALISATION	The total number of shares in issue multiplied by the market price of those shares.
CREDITORS	Money owed by a business to third parties.
DEBTORS	Money owed to a business by third parties.
DIVIDEND	The income that a business pays to individual shareholders, from after tax profits, usually both as an "Interim" and a "Final" paid after the year-end, and having been approved by shareholders.
FLOTATION	The act of "going public".
FREEHOLD	Owned outright i.e. not rented or leased.
INSTITUTIONS	Insurance companies, pension funds etc., as distinct from individual private investors.

INVESTMENT BANK	A bank which provides advice to businesses or individuals and which may or may not lend or invest money.
INVESTMENT TRUST	A company which owns shares in other quoted companies.
ISA (Individual Savings Account)	Into which a person can put a certain amount of money each year, (the Government stipulates the annual maximum allowable), with any interest or dividend income generated, or any Capital Gains made, free of all taxation except Inheritance Tax on death.
MARKET-MAKER	A firm whose business is the making of a market in shares i.e. like a wholesaler or middle-man to whom a stockbroker or bank will go to, to actually buy or sell shares.
PRICE EARNINGS RATIO	A business's capitalisation divided by its after-tax profits.
PROFIT	The difference between total turnover (sales or revenues) and total costs.
PROFIT AND LOSS ACCOUNT	Effectively showing the difference between items of income and items of expenditure.
PUBLIC COMPANY	A business which the general public can buy shares in as distinct from a "private" business which is owned by individuals or a family, and in which the public cannot buy shares.
STOCKBROKER	A firm whose business is the buying and selling of shares for investors.
TAKEOVER	Where one business buys another.
TURNOVER	The total value of products sold.
UNIT TRUST	An open-ended fund which owns shares in quoted companies.

An Ever-Changing Economy

Opportunities and Risks for Investors

When I started investing over sixty years ago, the UK Stock Market scene was very different. Then there were any number of quoted small regional Brewers to invest in, Clothing and Textile Companies, and many others in Aircraft Production, Motor Car Manufacture, Shipping, together with Rubber and Tea Plantation stocks, plus of course the many other categories which currently still exist. Today there are very few opportunities to invest in these aforementioned sectors. Some were consolidated via takeovers and mergers, particularly in Brewing, with many Textile and Clothing businesses going under, succumbing to cheaper competition from Third World countries. There are now hardly any individual Aircraft, Motor-Manufacturing or Shipping companies in the UK to invest in – most of these sectors are now dominated by very large international groups, and all Plantation companies have gone, primarily into the ownership of indigenous families overseas.

Over the years, there has been a range of publicly quoted businesses which came and went: Mail Order companies, Holiday Camp operators, Furniture Manufacturers, Newspaper Publishers, all providing opportunities for the investor for a time. Those who invested early in Supermarkets were rewarded, but today they are seen as mature, extremely competitive, and with very limited opportunities for further growth. In the 1980s, the privatisations of the Thatcher Conservative government brought many new companies to the Stock Market which previously had been state-owned: British Telecom, British Gas,

BP, Electricity and Rail, Steel and Water companies, providing mixed fortunes for investors, albeit significantly increasing the number of individuals owning shares. However some of the smaller privatisations like Amersham and Associated British Ports delivered substantial profits for the shrewd and patient. Historically Banks and Insurance companies were seen as safe and reliable, but the financial crisis of 2008 ended all that, although more recently they have been rebuilding profitability and reputations.

In my early investing days there were numerous small public property companies, both residential and commercial, to invest in, but consolidation has seen most morph into today's much larger property groups, although new niche openings have arisen in Care Homes, Self-Storage and Student Accommodation.

If we look more globally we see a growing world population, rising standards of living, and most people particularly in the Western world living longer. Common sense tells us that large international Food, Drink and Household Products groups like the Swiss Nestlé, America's Coca-Cola, Colgate, and Procter & Gamble, the Anglo-Dutch Unilever, and the UK's Diageo should all progress. Healthcare is an obvious growth area – over the decades larger Drug manufacturers have prospered, handsomely rewarding investors, but their days of easy profits are long gone with new drug discoveries being very expensive and Governments taking a much tougher line on prices. The danger of smoking has changed the perception of Tobacco stocks from growth to slow decline. Expanding populations need more houses, but housebuilding in the UK has historically been very cyclical although in recent years Government incentives have brought increased profits for Housebuilders. The development of the Internet and that of mobile phones have led to profound changes to so many lives and businesses. Huge American companies like Apple, Facebook, Google, Microsoft, Netflix and more recently Uber have delivered multi-billion pound fortunes for their founders and big profits for early stage investors, and of course, the giant Amazon has transformed retailing for ever. Had one stood back and thought about the economic and commercial consequences of Amazon's growth (which I sadly did not!), one could have foreseen the obvious beneficiaries e.g. Packaging Manufacturers and Delivery Logistics, plus the associated massive warehousing complexes. But, on the negative side, the losers have been the traditional high street Retailers, as has been well publicised. The New World of the Internet/home computers/iPads/mobile phones and their related software technologies have spawned a plethora of new commercial activities in Banking, Gambling, Games, Media Downloading and Streaming, and Travel/Hotel booking, plus developments in Cyber Security to counter hacking and fraud.

For the next generation of investors there are certain to be new exciting opportunities ahead – in Renewable Energy and Climate Change as we focus on a cleaner and more environmentally friendly planet, in Artificial Intelligence, Healthcare, Robotics, and Space etc. Investment opportunities are ever changing with new businesses arising as others inevitably decline.

Twelve Recommendations to help you invest profitably and successfully, and to avoid losses

1. Endeavour to buy shares on modest valuations – hopefully with a reasonable dividend yield, single figure or low double figure Price Earnings Ratios and/or a discount to Net Asset Value.
2. Ignore the overall level of the Stock Market – avoid making judgements on the world macro outlook – leave that to commentators and economists (who are invariably wrong!) Focus on your own particular stock selection.
3. Be prepared to hold the shares you buy for a minimum of five years and ideally ten plus.
4. Try to understand the company' business – look it up on the web – perhaps ask the company registrars or the company secretary to send you a copy of the last Annual Report, as a prospective shareholder.
5. Ignore minor share price movements when deciding to buy. If you like the company don't be put off because the shares have risen a few pence more than when you first alighted upon them. Looking back, say five years hence, you will have either done very well or not, and if you have made a mistake hopefully you will have sold and taken a loss and moved on (see 11 Stop-losses).
6. Seek established companies with a record of making profits and paying dividends. Avoid "start-ups" or biotech and exploration/mining stocks, or construction businesses,

which are all inherently risky. Remember the secret of investment success is to avoid losses.

7. Look for moderately optimistic or better Chairman's/ Chief Executive's most recent comments.

8. Focus on conservative, cash-rich companies or those with a low level of debt (borrowings).

9. Ensure that the Directors have meaningful shareholdings in the companies they are managing i.e. you are making sure that they have faith and belief in the businesses they are running. The last Annual Report should contain a list Directors' holdings.

10. Look for a stable Board with infrequent directorate changes. Similarly, with professional advisors like auditors, solicitors, bankers and brokers etc.

11. Face-up to mistakes, perhaps apply a 20% "Stop-loss" i.e. if you buy a share for 100p and its falls to 80p sell it and re-invest elsewhere, unless there are extenuating circum-stances. No one gets it right every time. However, if the overall level of the Stock Market falls ignore this "Stop-loss" rule.

12. Retain profitable shareholdings – hopefully to grow even more. Avoid the temptation to realise a quick profit. If you are invested in a good growing company which you like, which regularly increases its profits and dividends, stay aboard. The biggest mistake private investors make is too frequently chopping and changing – moving from share to share – stay put for bigger long-term profits!

TO LEARN MORE OR MAKE YOUR FIRST INVESTMENT

ASSOCIATION OF INVESTMENT COMPANIES – will provide details of all quoted Investment Trusts – www.theaic.co.uk

BANKS – most banks will undertake Stock Market transactions for their customers.

BOOKSHOPS – most bookshops will stock books on the Stock Market/Investment.

COMPANY'S ANNUAL REPORT – obtainable from its Company Secretary or Registrars.

COMPANY REFS – (Really Essential Financial Statistics) – online and hard copy information on all quoted companies via subscription – www.companyrefs.co.uk

IFA (Independent Financial Advisor) – a professionally qualified and regulated person who provides advice on a broad range of investments and on an individual's financial affairs

THE INVESTMENT ASSOCIATION – details of all Unit Trusts -www.theinvestmentassociation.org

MELLO – organises events/conferences/company presentations for private investors – www.melloevents.com

NEWSPAPERS – most have City/Business sections.

SHARESOC – the leading membership body for private investors (Information, campaigns, company visits etc.) – www.sharesoc.org

THE STOCK EXCHANGE – will provide a list of all Stockbrokers and their contact details and up-to-date share prices – mostly available online – www.londonstockexchange.com

STOCKOPEDIA – independent analysis of shares and data tools, via subscription – www.stockopedia.com

WEBSITES – all publicly quoted companies will have their own website, usually with a link to an "Investor Relations" section.

WEEKLY PUBLICATIONS – *The Investors Chronicle* (I have read for over 50 years!) - www.investorschronicle.co.uk; *Shares Magazine* also online - www.sharesmagazine.co.uk

BIONOTE

JOHN LEE is regarded as one of the UK's leading private investors having bought his first shares sixty years ago. He was one of the earliest to recognise the long-term potential of PEPs, the forerunner of ISAs when they were launched in 1987 and was judged to be the first ISA "millionaire" in 2003. He has written over 250 articles for *FT Money* and has given numerous lectures and interviews on his investment philosophy as a long-term "value" investor. In 2014 Pearsons published his well-received *How to Make a Million – Slowly: my guiding principles from a lifetime of successful investing*. He is a Chartered Accountant with a wide experience of investment banking and business and is Patron of ShareSoc, the leading body lobbying and campaigning on behalf of private investors. From 1979-92 he was a Member of Parliament, during this period he was both a Defence and Tourism Minister. A former High Sheriff of Greater Manchester, he sits as a member of the House of Lords as Lord Lee of Trafford and lives in Richmond, Surrey.

CPSIA information can be obtained
at www.ICGtesting.com
Printed in the USA
BVHW080009270520
580336BV00003B/182

9 781786 235206